# THE EARLY YEARS

## SASQUATCH SENIOR COMMUNITY
### BOOK 3

## PATRICK TALMADGE

HANGAR 1 PUBLISHING

# 1

## GU IS FOUND

Gu's early life started off normal for a Sasquatch kid. He was born and raised in the woods along the Tomoka River. Until his $3^{rd}$ year nothing was unusual, but then his life changed forever. Gu was playing near the river with the fellow Sasquatch kids when he saw a tree bent over, which he thought he could run up. Sasquatch don't normally climb trees because of their size and weight, but Gu was just a kid and didn't weigh much. He was also a rambunctious kid who thought running up the tree would be a lot of fun. Gu was no tree expert, so he did not notice that the tree he was running up was dead. He also hadn't paid attention to the fact the tree was overhanging the river. He had almost reached the top branch he was trying to grab when he heard a loud crack, and he began to fall.

It was 5 AM on a sweltering August morning as KO walked to the shoreline of the Tomoka River in Ormond Beach. It had been an unusually hot summer, but the last few weeks were even worse. KO had been getting up before the sun came up and cooked him in its afternoon heat. It was still quite dark, so a flashlight was needed just to get down to the shoreline, and today was definitely a day he was grateful he had one. As he approached the shoreline, he began hearing the sound of something splashing in the water. KO had seen a lot of strange things in the water and knew he should approach cautiously. He shined his flashlight back and forth out in the water until he found the source of the splashing.

KO thought he would find a gator or manatee from the sounds of the splashing, but he was not prepared for what he saw. A small ball of fur was trying to hold onto a log 15 feet from the shore. There was no way to know what it was or if it could hurt him, but KO couldn't stand the thought of any sort of being in distress, or worse, dying, so he jumped in. Later, he would question his decision since dawn was the alligators' favorite hunting time, and his boat was only 50 feet downstream and already in the water.

KO was so excited he sprinted the last 20 feet, then jumped hard, putting him about three feet from the log when he hit the water. He was close enough that he only needed a few strokes to reach the log. Once he grabbed the log, he slowly pulled himself towards this struggling ball of fur. He'd had to drop his flashlight so he could barely see an outline of the creature on the log in front of him. KO gently started saying are you OK in a whisper voice that you would say to a scared puppy. Before he could react, a small, furry hand reached out and grabbed his shirt. Then two furry little arms wrapped around his neck, and he was being hugged, while the wet ball of fur was cooing like a baby.

For some reason, after all the drama, KO thought this was funny and began laughing gently. Here he was, at 5 AM in dark, floating in the Tomoka River, with some sort of baby monkey hugging his neck. The little thing was beginning to relax after he reached the shoreline and sat in the sand, but it kept hugging him tightly. KO's flashlight was about 10 feet away but was shining enough light their way that some details of his armful of wet fur became visible. It was definitely some sort of monkey, except its feet seemed almost human, just bigger and fur-covered. Its hands looked like human hands, and again, the only difference was they were bigger and covered with soft fur.

The little thing must have been exhausted from being in the water because it began falling asleep in his arms as he walked. The little monkey thing was asleep when KO reached his cabin. KO was grateful he had left his dog in its cage when he went out to work. His dog is very curious, and KO was afraid it would get too close to the river and be grabbed by an alligator or bit by a snake in the dark, so he kept him in his cage while he worked.

KO took the little monkey thing inside and laid it on the sofa near the door. He decided to leave the door open while the little thing slept on the sofa in the event it woke up and became afraid. Having the door open would have left it an escape route so it wouldn't be as worried. KO sat on the edge of the bed, looking at the little monkey, wondering where it came from. The more he looked at the face of the little monkey, the more he realized it looked less like a baby gorilla and more like a hairy human.

KO had been sitting on the bed watching the little monkey thing when he fell asleep. He wasn't sure if it was because he'd been getting up early to work hard or the excitement of finding the monkey floating on the log, but he fell asleep watching the little thing. When he woke up, the first thing he noticed was that the little monkey was gone. The second thing he noticed was his dog was out of its cage. The third thing KO noticed was the monkey and the dog weren't gone. They were snuggled together next to him.

The only thing KO could figure out was that the monkey thing had let the dog out of its cage, and the two of them had snuggled into bed with him. Well, at least he didn't have to worry about the dog bothering the monkey anymore. KO had found his dog

Pebbles by the river when he was just a 5-week-old puppy. He wasn't sure how the poor puppy ended up there, but Pebbles had been his daily companion since then. Wow, he thought. It had been three years since little Pebbles came into his life as a gift from the Tomoka River, and now this furry little monkey had been sent to him by the river. As KO was marveling at his dog and this new furry arrival, snuggling, it dawned on him that he better call his wife immediately.

He needed food for the new guy, and he should find a way to tell her gently that he now had a monkey. While dialing his wife, KO started wondering if this monkey thing was a relative of one of the monkeys that escaped while they were shooting the Tarzan movies here in the Ormond swamps years ago. It was 9:00 in the morning, so he knew his wife was up and that the grocery store would also be open, so now he had to figure out a way to have his wife go to the store to get what he needed without her asking too many questions.

By the time his wife answered the phone, KO had decided to tell her a small lie that he had found another puppy and needed milk and a bottle to feed it with. He was trying to figure out how to ask her to also pick up a big bunch of bananas when he suddenly came up with another small lie and told her he was going to try to catch catfish in a new way that his buddy Gator had told him about. His wife laughed when he told her about Gator's method for catching catfish, and she replied that the only thing Gator had ever caught was a hangover. The last thing he needed was a book on apes and monkeys from the library, and that story would have to be a doozy. He was going to tell her that one of the men in town thought he had seen a monkey when he was deep in the swamp a couple of weeks ago, and they needed a book to see if they could figure out what kind of monkey it was.

KO was worried after he hung up from talking to his wife,

trying to figure out how he was going to tell her about the monkey. Well, if there is a God above, he was listening today because when his wife came by after shopping, she was in a hurry to get to her sister's house, so she never got out of the car. While KO was grabbing the bags, his wife reminded him she would be gone for the next week to help take care of her sister's new baby. KO was relieved when she reminded him because it meant he had a whole week to get used to his new monkey friend before he had to tell his wife. He watched his wife drive away, totally relieved that he had some time to work things out.

When KO walked into the house, he noticed his dog Pebbles and the monkey baby on the floor playing quietly. He watched the two gently playing on the floor for a minute when they finally noticed him standing there in the doorway. Pebbles looked up, and his tail immediately started wagging, but he stayed right where he was with the little baby monkey. KO was sure Pebbles was staying close to the baby to protect it. The little monkey thing looked up, seemed to smile, then stood up, ran over to KO, wrapped its arms around his leg, and hugged him tightly. After a long leg hug, the little guy looked up, then held his arms up, asking to be picked up.

KO looked down at that cute little monkey face, which honestly, he thought looked very human-like. Then he reached down and picked it up. The little guy hugged KO tightly, like when he had first saved him from the river. KO had a daughter about this guy's size, and this little guy hugged just like a normal human kid. He was beginning to wonder what this guy was. Was he a chimpanzee, a gorilla, or some other kind of ape that he didn't know about? KO hugged the little guy close, picked up the great ape and monkey book his wife had brought, then walked over to the couch and sat down. Pebbles came over and sat beside the little monkey like he was protecting him again. KO sat on the sofa with his two fur-covered friends and opened the book.

Pebbles and the monkey climbed down onto the floor and began playing like kids and dogs always do while KO read the book. No ape or monkey in the book looked like his new friend. The little guy looked like a gorilla with longer legs and feet like a human. This thing had human-shaped feet, but its feet were much bigger than those of a human child of the same size. He would need to check out more books or see someone at a zoo.

KO couldn't keep calling it a little monkey, so he needed to come up with a name for this little guy. If this little guy had been an alligator, he would have called it Wally because Wally Gator was his favorite cartoon. The more he thought about it, the more he decided he was going to call it Wally anyway. Wally Gator is a swamp creature in the cartoons, and this is definitely a swamp creature, so I'm going to call him Wally from now on, thought KO.

# 2

---

# THE FIRST WEEK WITH WALLY

The first week with Wally would have been tough if it hadn't been for pebbles. Like all toddlers, Wally needed constant attention, and KO was just too busy trying to build the marina to be there for Wally 24/7. Pebbles, being only three years old, was still acting like a puppy, so having a young playmate was exactly what he needed as well. For the most part, the two were inseparable, except when Wally got a chance to ride around on KO's shoulders. KO wasn't really sure how old Wally was, but he was about the size of a tall 5-year-old, just a bit heavier. If this is a young one of its kind, I wonder how big the daddy is? he thought.

Day one went fairly smoothly, and the little guy picked up potty training quickly. At first, KO took Wally outside in the grass when he thought nature might be calling him. Once KO felt Wally knew what it meant when he said, 'let's go potty' KO began teaching him to go in the inside toilet. To be honest, Wally was so fascinated with the inside plumbing, it was quite easy to get him to use the toilet. Since Wally was so small, KO taught him to always sit down when he went to the bathroom, and hopefully, sitting would also keep the floors a bit cleaner.

As it turned out, Wally was not interested in the milk and didn't need a bottle, so he learned to use a cup right away. KO was amazed. He was thankful that he had asked his wife for a lot of bananas, and Wally really seemed to like the bananas. The book his wife had brought him listed the things that great apes and monkeys eat, which gave KO Some good ideas on what to feed Wally. Luckily, he had stocked the cabin with lots of food in preparation for his wife being gone for a week. He also usually had shelves in the back room with supplies for the people who lived on their boats along the river.

After laying everything out that KO knew an ape like Wally could eat, he had 6 boxes of apples, a full bin of corn on the cob, 150 pounds of potatoes, and a 20-gallon bucket of mixed nuts. There was enough to keep Wally fed for a month, let alone the week he needed to plan how to break the information to his wife. KO wasn't sure what his wife's response would be, but his daughter would be in heaven. It was obvious that Wally was gentle from how he and Pebbles got along and how he enjoyed being held and cuddled. His daughter and Wally were going to be best friends.

KO was thinking how much he wanted to know what Wally was when he remembered one of the River people, a man named Cooper, who was living on a houseboat up the river, told him one day, months passed, that he'd been a Florida State park ranger until a gator bit his foot off. KO decided anybody deep enough into the swamp to get their foot bitten off would surely know if there were any big monkeys in the swamps of the Tomoka River. Once he knew Wally would behave himself and was calm enough, KO would cruise up the river and ask Cooper if he'd ever heard of monkeys living in the swamps.

If fate were a bag of money, I'd be rich, KO thought, because just at that moment, he heard Cooper, the ex-park ranger, motoring his skiff towards the dock. It was an unmistakable-sounding boat. The guy had put a small steam-powered motor in his skiff, so he would never need gas or diesel fuel. He could burn coal, wood, or trash. The sound of a steam motor was definitely unique and would never be confused with an outboard motor sound. Cooper was very eclectic but nice. He lived off the land by fishing and collecting fruits and nuts. He would sell the extra he caught or collected for cash, which is one reason KO had 20 gallons of nuts in his storeroom.

The river community was a tight bunch that didn't trust outsiders or governments. They all worked together closely to make sure everyone was safe and healthy, which is why KO had so much stock in the back storeroom. Some of the river people, as they were known, living along the Tomoka were retired locals who wanted to return to a simpler existence without the trouble city life brings. Most of them were tough locals whose family had been living along the Tomoka for 5 generations or more and made a good living trapping and hunting. However, most of the money they made was from their community fishing efforts. Many people who lived along the river worked together to bring their fish catch into the town market, and everyone profited.

KO met the incoming boat at the dock and greeted his friend Cooper. Once the boat was tied up, KO asked Cooper if he'd sit and talk for a while and share some fresh sweet tea because he had a few questions. Cooper told him he wasn't one to turn down sweet tea offered on a hot day and followed KO over to the covered porch off the cabin. KO Started the conversation slowly, with normal pleasantries, like how have you been doing? How's your foot? How's the heat getting to you, and have you ever seen any kind of monkey in the swamp?

Cooper's eyes nearly flew out his head when KO asked him if he'd ever seen any kind of monkey in the swamp. KO could tell by the way Cooper was now looking at him that Cooper must have seen something like a monkey himself. KO took a chance and told Cooper how he found this little monkey thing floating down the river on a log. KO went on to tell him how it looked like a gorilla with almost human feet and that the hairy face was almost human-looking. Before KO could say more about Wally, Cooper began staring into space and talking.

**3**
———————

# COOPER'S RECOLLECTION OF THE ATTACK

I ain't never told anyone this story Cooper began. I was afraid that if I told what I saw in the swamp, and how I made it back alive, people would think I was crazy. KO, you have lived here your whole life, and you know it would be impossible for a man to travel almost 10 miles through the swamp with a fever and hurt foot in mere hours. Well, it would be impossible for me to have made it out alone. I had help, and I would have gone to my grave without saying a thing if you hadn't asked about seeing a monkey.

It happened over 30 years ago when I was still young, wet behind the ears, and still had 2 feet. I was up the Tomoka River deep in the swamp, looking for a cow-killing gator. One of the farmers had already lost 4 cows to the monster, and the tracks were bigger than anything anyone had ever seen. We estimated this gator must be over 20 feet long. There were 8 of us in 4 boats searching. We didn't have walkie-talkies or shortwave radios in those days, so we used our rifles as signal guns. Three shots meant come now, it's an emergency, two shots meant you found it, and one shot was to be used every 30 minutes so we knew where each other was.

The swamp was thick with hundreds of small channels, so most of the time, the boats were within 100 or 200 feet of each other. The single shot helped keep the boats in a cluster for safety. It was often possible to see the boats if you were in the driver's tower. These swamp boats needed a tower much like a lifeguard tower so the driver could see dangerous sunken logs and, hopefully, big gators.

All the men in the boats carried a custom 45 caliber semi-automatic rifle for this hunt. Normally when hunting a killer gator, the rangers carried a 22-caliber or even a 30-caliber rifle, but with a Gator this huge, no one was going to take a chance. Not that anyone had a chance when that monster finally showed up. I was down on the deck of the boat with one of the senior Rangers with more experience driving the boat from the tower when we heard screaming and the sound of the boat being turned over. I could hear a few people yelling around us, but I couldn't see them because I was too low. I heard my driver yelling to one of the other boat drivers that we were going to be coming their way and to stay where they were. Then my driver yelled down to me to hold on tight, and we took off at full speed.

As I said, I was new to being a park ranger and had never been in one of these boats at full power. I also didn't know that these air boats could go over short marsh brush and even small logs, which is how I ended up on land while the boat continued going forward finally into the channel water. The boat had hit a log that was too big, which made the air boat jump three feet in the air and pitched me out at 30 miles per hour.

I was barely conscious, sprawled out on top of the brush, but I can remember the far-off sounds of boats crashing and people screaming. I fell unconscious and wasn't sure how long I'd been out but by the time I came to, the light in the swamp was beginning to fade. I could feel that I'd hit my head, but I wasn't bleeding, so I wasn't worried about dying quickly. Now, my first duty was to find the other rangers and the boats so we could get out of the swamp.

After a wobbly start, I was able to stand up by using the brush around me. My goal was to make my way to one of the big trees. I needed to find a high spot if I was going to find the other Rangers and boats. If I couldn't find anybody soon, I was going to need the high ground of the tree to stay safe from rising tide waters, alligators, and the many predators that might be prowling at night in the swamp for their meal.

I saw a perfect palm tree that had fallen against a huge old oak tree. The angle of the palm tree looked so shallow I could almost walk up it, so I made my way to the palm tree. Just as I thought, I could walk right up the palm tree like it was a ramp. Once I reached the oak, I climbed high so I could scan the surrounding areas for the rangers and boats. I had heard no sounds since I came too, but expected to see my fellow rangers gathered together, preparing to search for me, or at least be bedding down for the night. I was shocked at what I saw.

The only thing I could find were pieces and parts of boats floating around in the various channels surrounding the oak tree I was in. I was grateful to be holding on tight when I saw the first of the Rangers floating motionless in the canal. The site was so shocking that I wretched until my stomach was empty. When I was able to compose myself enough, I slowly scanned the areas around the boat wreckage, searching for survivors, hopefully, if not then bodies. I was able to locate two more bodies, and much to my horror, what I believed were body parts, and while I was searching, I found what had caused all the horrific destruction of life.

I was blessed that I was not bleeding, or down in the water with the other Rangers, because swimming in the channel with one of the Rangers in its mouth was the biggest alligator I had ever seen. It wasn't just the biggest alligator I'd ever seen; this alligator was the biggest alligator ever recorded, and it was almost 25 feet in length. I'm not sure why it happened, but this gigantic alligator destroyed all four boats and killed the seven men that were in them. It was by the grace of God I was thrown from the boat and landed in the dense brush, or I would have suffered the same fate as my fellow Rangers.

I stayed up in that oak tree for the next two days while the killer 25-foot gator rummaged through the four boats, ensuring it had found the last of the Rangers. I had gotten out of the tree a few times when nature called and tried to search the shoreline for any lost rations or gear I could use when I tried to make my way out of the swamp. I knew we were at least 10 miles in, and to my reckoning, I didn't have much chance of making it out alive, but I wasn't going to give up without trying. I knew the way to the road almost 10 miles away, but it meant crossing some of the thickest jungle and croc-infested water, assuming I could avoid the monster that killed my fellow rangers.

It took 4 hours to go a difficult 300 feet through the dense brush, only to come up upon an open channel of water 50 feet across. There was no way to cross this channel without swimming, which meant swimming in alligator-infested waters. I had been sitting dejected, looking out over the water for almost an hour, when a palm tree came crashing down across the channel and landed just 20 feet from me. My first thought was to hide, thinking the giant crocodile was back and now hunting me. Unknown to me, a Sasquatch had seen me, watched my struggles with the gator, and decided to help. I lay hidden in the brush for 10 minutes without hearing a sound and decided to try to find out what had just happened.

I'm not sure how it happened, whether it was the crocodile, a freak wind, or an act of God, but the palm tree had fallen completely across the channel and formed a perfect bridge for me to walk across. It was a blessing I wasn't going to pass up, but I still had over 9 miles of the same kind of terrain to go through before I got back to civilization. After cautiously crossing the fallen palm tree, I found what could only be described as a game trail, which meant my travels, as long as they went in my direction, were going to be a lot easier. I don't know how long the game trail had been there, but it was well-worn, and it seemed like whatever was using it wasn't comfortable walking in the water. Whoever it was, it had laid a path of logs across every channel, around every pond, and marshy ground. The interesting part was that some of the trees and logs were very recent, so recent it was like it had only been days or minutes since they had been laid down.

It wasn't until after my recovery in the hospital that I realized that something had helped me. It helped by pushing down trees and sometimes laying logs down, so I could traverse the deepest swamp and cross channels. I was tired, scared, and thought maybe I'd seen things, but I would have sworn I saw a big guy deep in the shadows watching me a few times.

Late the first day, I stepped over a log 12 inches in diameter when a small alligator bit my foot. The darn gator was only about 2 feet long, but it was big enough to bite through my boot and draw blood. As soon as the little guy bit me, he took off into the water, and I never saw him again. I knew I wasn't hurt badly, but I was worried that the bleeding might attract predators. Alligators weren't the only predators in the swamps, so I needed to stop and bandage it up. I decided to climb a tree so I would be safer. I didn't want to be caught on the ground with one boot off if an alligator or a Panther got wind of the blood.

The oaks in the swamp can grow pretty big, and they're tough old trees, but luckily, some of the branches are hanging low enough that they're easy to get into, even with a hurt foot. I hadn't been able to get a very large selection of bandages and gauze, but I had enough to bandage up the bites on my foot. The big problem was alligators' mouths can be pretty dirty, and infections can set in, which normally wouldn't be a problem, but I didn't have any antibiotics with me, and out in this wet swamp with wet boots, I could be in a world of hurt without the correct medicine. I knew I needed to hurry, so as soon as I got my foot bandaged up, I started off again.

Because of the easy trails and logs, I made pretty good time for the rest of the day, but by the time it was starting to get dark and I began searching for a tree to sleep in, I realized I was starting to feel sick, and I was beginning to worry an infection was setting in on my foot.

When I woke up the next morning, I realized it was the 4th day since the giant Gator attacked and the second day hiking since I started back. After two days of walking in the swamp and after that small alligator bite, I was starting to have trouble with my foot. It was swelling and starting to hurt something nasty, and I was afraid to take the boot off for fear I wouldn't be able to get it back on, and then I wouldn't be able to walk.

I'm not sure of how long after I got bit when I finally couldn't go on anymore. I saved enough energy to climb a small tree, to get myself off the ground and out of any alligator's reach. I knew that no matter what I did or how high I climbed, I wouldn't ever get out of a Panthers reach, so I had to take my chances and find a safe spot, because I knew I wouldn't last much longer. I finally found a cluster of branches shaped like a cupped hand at least 10 feet off the ground, which gave me enough support and protection that if I passed out, I wouldn't fall out of the tree.

I don't remember anything after settling into the tree. I have fleeting memories of being gently picked up from the tree and carried like a baby. There were times I remember thick fur and a kind of heavy animal smell. More than once, I seemed to remember looking up and seeing what looked like a giant ape looking down at me, seemingly smiling. For some reason, I wasn't uncomfortable or scared. I felt almost safe and comforted. I don't think I traveled more than a mile before I had to settle into that tree. Somehow, over a matter of hours, I made it the final eight or more miles out of that dense swamp, which should have taken me at least a week traveling if I survived at all. All I know is they found me lying next to the road unconscious and took me to the hospital.

One of the weirdest parts is, when they found me, my foot was wrapped up in leaves with some sort of plant mud poultice covering the infected bite. The emergency room doctor said whoever had put that poultice on my leg most likely saved my life. The plants they used were natural antibiotics and were strong enough to keep the infection from traveling further, saving my life but not my foot.

The infection had done so much damage to the foot that the doctor had to amputate it to save my life. It's kind of embarrassing to say you've lost your foot from an infection, so I always say a gator bit it off because that sounds better. I feel a massive amount of guilt, being I was the only one that survived out of the eight Rangers that went into the swamp. I think that's why I chose to live on the river. It's my way of staying close to them.

# 4

## COOPER MEETS WALLY

KO watched Cooper sit silently, thinking deeply after he had finished his story. After a few minutes of silence, KO asked Cooper to excuse him for a minute while he went to get something for Cooper to see. Cooper was so deep in thought when KO went into the cabin that he didn't notice, nor did he notice when KO came back outside with a friend walking at his side. It wasn't until the two of them were standing directly in front of him that Cooper registered their presence, and then he slowly stood.

For the longest time, he didn't move a muscle or make a sound, then Cooper looked at Wally, then at KO, back to Wally, again turned to KO and said OH my god, they are real. I have spent 20 years of my life thinking I was crazy, and now here's proof I wasn't.

You know, now that I get a good look at this thing, I am thinking it has to be one of them Big Foot things, that Patterson guy up north in Oregon a few years back filmed, but this one must still be a baby, said Cooper. I think the Native Americans called them Sasquatch, and I can see where the nickname Bigfoot came from. Cooper said and laughed a bit.

Wally had been staying close to KO's leg while they stood near Cooper because Cooper was only the second human he'd ever seen. When Cooper held his hand out, Wally slowly took a couple of small steps closer and reached out to touch Cooper's hand. Cooper remained perfectly still, because he knew the little guy was nervous, but while Wally was touching his hand, Cooper was feeling so happy himself that he was smiling big. Once Wally saw Cooper's smile, he instantly knew everything was all right and actually reached his arms up, asking to be picked up.

Cooper eagerly obliged Wally and picked him up. Wally instantly hugged him tight, while Cooper looked at KO, saying this might be the greatest moment in my life. After watching these two, who had never met, greet each other so tenderly, it was obvious they would be friends for life. As it turns out, later in life, Wally and Cooper's friendship kept building, and they even worked together sometimes, gathering food or fishing.

KO's wife still wouldn't be home for five or six days, so he and Cooper spent every day working with Wally, trying to make sure that he understood certain commands so that when he met KO's wife and daughter, they would be sure it was safe. They needed to know that Wally wasn't aggressive. As it turned out, Wally did not have any anger issues. Very little scared or upset him, but he had an incredible sense of humor. Wall's favorite joke was to scare Cooper by saying boo.

Wally was able to say a few of the simple words. He could say Boo, food, and water, but he couldn't say Cooper, which Cooper thought was funny because it always came out Pooper. When Wally called Cooper, Pooper, Cooper would laugh, and say Wally was trying to tease him.

# 5

## WALLY MEETS KO'S WIFE AND DAUGHTER

When he got up, KO realized it had been eight days since he found Wally floating in the river. Wally was doing great, but today would be a monumental test of how he reacted to new people because his wife and daughter would be coming down to the cottage in an hour. KO was sure Wally was going to be fine with his wife and daughter. He knew his daughter was going to be in heaven with Wally. He just wasn't sure how his wife was going to react. Just then, he heard Cooper's boat coming down on the river. He went over to the stove and started the coffee.

By the time Cooper got his boat tied up and reached the cabin, the coffee was almost done. Wally had been sleeping soundly in the little hammock that he loved to sleep in when he heard Cooper's boat, got up, and ran out to greet him. After coming into the cabin and talking for about 30 minutes, Wally stood up and looked out the window because he'd heard something. Turns out that something was his wife and daughter driving down the driveway, which meant the show was about to begin. KO looked over at Cooper and said I'm really glad you're here for this one, buddy.

Wally knew he was going to meet new people and needed to be calm. Two weeks earlier, KO would never have thought it possible to teach a wild animal so much, but then Wally is almost as intelligent as a human.

KO wasn't wrong about his daughter loving Wally and Wally loving her. The moment the two young ones saw one another, they ran to one another, hugged, and then immediately sat on the floor to look at the stuffed toy Wally was carrying. KO's wife was a different story. She froze in place. In fact, KO was surprised she didn't even move when the two young ones ran together and hugged. Finally, after a minute, she looked over at KO and Cooper, shaking her head back and forth, and said, 'I can't believe this'.

Wally and KO's daughter sat on the floor playing like normal 5-year-olds. They would play a little bit, laugh at nothing, and pretty much simply enjoy each other 's company.

Finally, KO's wife said, "At least now I know I'm not crazy".

KO and Cooper both looked at her with weird, questioning eyes, And she said let me tell you what I saw. KO's wife sat down in a chair and began tspeaking about an incident five years earlier while she was just starting labor with their daughter Sandy.

KO's wife recounted how five years ago, she could tell she was starting to go into labor, so she stopped here at the cabin on the way home from work, and that's when she saw the thing. She pulled in the back driveway and parked behind the cabin. She needed to grab a bag she had left on the front porch earlier, so she turned on the floodlight and went out the front door. What she saw by the dock made her stop dead in her tracks.

Directly under the light by the dock was a huge bear, or she thought it was a bear, until it stood up and turned towards her. What, at first, she thought was a bear rummaging around the dock turned out to be some sort of ape that had to be at least 7 feet tall, and it was staring right at her. Reflectively, she wrapped her arms around her belly, protecting her unborn baby. The moment she did, the giant ape thing turned towards her and wrapped its arms around its own distended belly, and now she could see that the ape thing in front of her was actually a female, and it was also pregnant. The female ape looked at her and actually smiled. Then the ape caressed her belly while rocking her arms back and forth, slowly turning and walking into the jungle.

KO's wife finished talking, silently stared at the two young ones playing, and then exclaimed that this one must be the child of the one I saw five years ago. But where is its mom she said as she walked over to Sandy and Wally. The kids stopped playing, and Wally took one look at Sandy's mom, smiled, and stood up with his arms up, asking to be picked up.

KO's wife picked up Wally, then her daughter Sandy came over as well and wanted to be held. She sat for the longest time holding the two children of different species, both sweet and loving. While his wife held the two children, KO recanted how he found Wally floating down the Tomoka River a little over a week ago. He explained how he had been trying to teach him words and manners so that he could safely be around Sandy and her mom. He let them know how smart Wally seemed to be and that he had a great sense of humor.

Something seemed to change in Wally after he sat on KO's wife's lap with his daughter, Sandy. He seemed almost sad, but he was definitely quiet. Little Sandy noticed it, and she suggested maybe he was missing his mommy. KO's wife asked him if he had seen Wally's mother. KO admitted he had not seen Wally's mom or any other Sasquatch other than Wally.

"KO, I think you need to try to find out where Wally came from and reunite him with his family", KO's wife said.

"Honestly, after seeing him this way, I really think that's a great idea", said KO. "Cooper, you're going to have to tell me how far up the Tomoka you think this little guy came from, KO added.

# 6

## WALLY GOES HOME

Over the next few days, Cooper and KO prepared and outfitted a special boat KO had specially designed for hunting. The boat was a -built 18-foot-long, 6-foot-wide salt marsh skiff made of two super light but incredibly strong Kevlar canoes. KO had created a one-of-a-kind, 6-foot-wide catamaran saltmarsh boat. It even had a covered area for the pilot and a passenger. It also had a pop-up cover for sleeping at night or even bad weather. The pilot area was raised for better visibility and transformed into a bed for sleeping.

What was different about this boat was its propulsion system. KO wanted to be able to cruse the Tomoka silently, whether he was hunting or fishing. He also didn't want to be tied to the government or have to buy fuel, but Cooper's steam-powered boat was a bit too loud and smelled because he needed to burn wood or coal as fuel to heat the boiler.

First, he developed a peddle system that turned four small propellers. The propellers were positioned two on each side of the boat, and each operated independently from the others, giving maximum maneuverability. There was a prop on each corner of the boat, both in the front and in the back. The setup allowed for the boat to spin in circles, or if the area was too small, it could be shifted into reverse and back out.

Since KO didn't want to peddle up or against a tidal current, he added an electric motor to the chain his peddles turned. To power the electric motor, he used two big boat batteries. To charge the batteries, KO used four of the new solar panels they were now making and used them to make the covered area above the pilot. In the event the batteries died at night, KO added a small car generator that also ran off his chain, and he could charge the batteries while he peddled.

Once the boat systems had been checked dozens of times, the supplies loaded, goodbyes said, and hugs hugged, KO and Wally headed up the Tomoka River. Cooper thought it would take two or three days to get to where he thinks Wally's family lives, but maybe less if they were down closer when Wally fell in the river. Either way, the boat was outfitted with enough supplies for KO and Wally to be gone two weeks. They would head upstream for a week, and if they didn't find his family, they would head back downstream.

The Tomoka River is brackish and affected by tides. KO's plan was to peddle when he was riding with the tidal currents or at slack tide and use the electric motor when traveling against the currents. The first day of their travels went perfectly. KO peddled when it was easy and ran the motor when it wasn't. The boat wasn't as fast as a skiff with a gas motor, but it was silent, and they surprised many birds and gators as they silently came around a bend in the river. This was a perfect shakedown test for the boat, and it was passing with flying colors.

The second day went as smoothly as the first. Everything on the boat was working perfectly. Even the sleeping area worked great. The sleeping area needed to be raised and sealed at night to protect them from predators. A gator could climb on the boat's main deck, but not the sealed sleeping area. Also, the sleeping area was sealed well enough not even a snake could make it in. KO hated snakes, and that was one of his personal requirements. KO wasn't worried about the occasional bear since they would anchor away from the shore most nights, but sometimes the big cats could be dangerous. A hungry panther might try to go after Wally or even KO at night, so KO made special breathable tight weave Kevlar mesh sides that could keep mosquitoes out and stop a panther.

After breakfast, KO and Wally headed upstream. The tide was coming in, so the peddling was easy and required mostly steering and only slight peddling as they rode the tide upstream. Just before they were going to stop for lunch, Wally was looking out over the river when an animal call came from just upriver, which caused Wally to freeze and stare towards the call. Ten seconds later, there was another call, but this one was to our left on shore. Within 30 seconds, dozens of calls were coming from every direction, surrounding the boat.

Wally had been standing near the bow listening to the first calls, and then he joined the chorus of calls. I had never heard Wally raise his voice let alone yell, and boy was that little guy loud. Wally stopped calling and began staring into the brush to our right side. The noise behind the thick brush sounded like something huge was making a path towards them. The boat was a good 20 feet from shore, so KO wasn't worried about being attacked, but he was definitely curious about what could be making so much noise. There was no way to prepare to see something as incredible as an adult Sasquatch for the first time.

The Sasquatch that burst through the dense jungle brush was amazing. It was easily over 8-foot-tall and looked like it could turn over a car. KO was grateful they were out of reach because it looked upset and made plenty of scary noise. Ten feet away from the first Sasquatch, a second one came through the brush to the shoreline. The second Sasquatch was much shorter and lighter than the first. The second sasquatch was just under 7-foot-tall, which KO thought might be a female, after seeing the first one.

From Wally's reaction to the second Sasquatch, it was a female and not just any female, but it was his mother. Wally began jumping up and down, calling his mom. Wally ran over to KO, grabbed his hand, and pointed to the second Sasquatch. KO knew Wally wanted him to peddle the boat over, but he was afraid. The big male was still making deep, threatening sounds, and KO feared the female might get violent. KO made the hand sign he used with Wally which meant scared, and Wally suddenly relaxed. He gave KO a long hug, stood, and walked to the side of the boat closest to his mother.

Wally made sounds and hand signals towards his mom and the big male, and after a few tries, the two adult Sasquatch settled down and became silent. Wally made more gestures and sounds while they listened, and then he wrapped his arms around KO and hugged him tightly. The two Sasquatch seemed to understand and almost seemed to smile. There was a sand beach 50 feet further down the shore, which Walley pointed at and signaled for KO to head for. KO wasn't feeling 100 % confident, but he trusted Walley and peddled to the shoreline. Once the boat landed, Wally jumped out, pulled it up above the hightide line like KO had taught him, then turned to face the jungle and the sounds heading for them.

The big male first came into the small clearing and seemed to place himself close to KO, but not so close KO felt threatened. The female came out after the male was set, and once she was out of the brush, Wally rushed over to her. It was a beautiful reunion.

Wally was crying happy tears, and his mom was kissing his face and hugging him over and over. Wally finally broke the hug and pointed at KO.

KO was still sitting in his boat seat, but Wally was waving at him to get off the boat and meet his mom. KO could see that Wally's mom had a smile, but she was easily two feet taller than he was. She was also hundreds of pounds heavier, covered in fur, and those teeth were terrifying, but he slowly walked to Wally and his mother. When he was 10 feet away, Wally jumped down from his mom's arms, ran to KO, and held his arms up to have KO pick him up. KO picked Wally up and walked towards his mother.

Up close, Wally's mom was huge. She completely dwarfed KO. Walley's mom looked at the two of them standing there, and a big smile came across her face. Her smile made KO relax a little bit, so when she reached out and pulled them in for a hug, he didn't jump. While Wally's mother was hugging them, the big male stepped forward and stopped a few feet away.

Wally's mom released KO and Wally, and the two of them turned and faced the big male. Wally held his arms up to the big male, and he gently lifted Wally out of KO's arms. Wally hugged the big male for a long while, and the male seemed genuinely glad to see him, so KO assumed the male was Wally's father. While Wally was hugging the big male, more Sasquatch came out of the brush and stood on the sand beach. By the time they were all on the beach, there were six adult males, seven adult females, and five young Sasquatch. Wally had a mighty fine Sasquatch troupe, and they were very interested in KO.

Wally climbed down from the big male's arms and came back to KO's side while the other Sasquatch met him. They were very gentle but wanted to smell and feel his hair. KO's long, pre-mature gray hair was unique to them, and they seemed to like it. It was a bit unnerving to have an 8-foot-tall hairy beast with a mouth that could swallow a volleyball bend down and smell your head, but KO held his composure while they checked him out. When the last of Wally's troupe had greeted KO, the big male was the last to stand before him.

The big male looked at Wally, smiled at KO, gave him a big smile, then gently wrapped its arms around KO, picked him up, gave him a long hug, kissed him on the top of his head, then set KO down. Once KO was on the ground, the rest of the Sasquatch began making sounds like chanting, and then they all turned and headed back into the dense jungle. When the last of the Sasquatch troupe had entered the jungle, except Wally his mother and father the large male, Wally grabbed on to KO's arm, and tugged. It was obvious Wally wanted KO to follow them. So far, he felt safe, but following a bunch of giant apes into the jungle was about as much stress as KO could handle. Wally tugged on his arm one more time, so KO looked at Wally's mother and father, took a deep breath, reached into the boat, grabbed his backpack, and then followed them into the unknown.

# 7

## WALLY'S HOME

The trek from the river through the jungle took about 10 minutes. As KO stepped out of the jungle into a clearing, he was amazed at what he saw. The clearing was approximately 300 feet in diameter and 10 feet higher than the surrounding jungle ground. Moments before, as they began coming out of the jungle, they climbed a gentle ramp until they reached the top of this raised clearing, and then they went through a tall rock wall. Around the perimeter of the raised ground was a rock wall approximately 10 feet high, and it also had a wood gate that closed watertight when needed. KO learned later that the wall and raised area were so that the village would be safe in the event of floods.

Mounds were around the perimeter of the circle and along the rock wall. The mounds were made of rock and dirt walls at least 10 feet tall with trees growing at the top of the wall. They were live trees planted side by side and woven together as they grew, creating a living wall and roof that looked like a basket. From the outside, the houses looked like an overgrown brush-covered rock wall. The walls were so well built, and the trees woven so tight that the roof and walls were waterproof, and the whole house was hurricane-proof too.

On the inside of the mounds, the walls were neat and trimmed. Each wall had an opening big enough for a full-grown Sasquatch to walk through standing upright. Each of the openings had a woven grass and stick door that could be closed to keep the weather out. There was one grass and moss mat that was the communal bed in each home. The Sasquatch are very social, so touch and hugs are their favorite forms of showing affection.

KO was glad he wore his backpack because, from the looks of it, he would be spending the night here. Wally brought him to what he could only assume was his house and showed him the sleeping mat, so KO put his backpack down next to it. Wally was excited to show KO everything in his house. Wally showed him their table made from an old wooden wire spool, and on the table was a large metal bowl with fruit and nuts in it. Next to the bowl was a 2-gallon metal can with water. Wally was very proud of their things, and after being with KO for eight days in the cabin, it must seem a bit rustic, but still, Wally was proud to show his house off. When he was done showing KO his house, Wally headed back outside, and KO followed him.

Once outside, KO noticed that the whole Sasquatch troupe had gathered in the center of the clearing, and Wally was taking him there, too. As they approached, KO could see that everyone in the troupe had brought food and was laying it out on little woven grass mats. KO assumed they were celebrating Wally's return. After looking at the woven baskets and mats, it occurred to KO that the Sasquatch had made them themselves. Obviously, the Sasquatch were quite intelligent. The woven baskets and woven mats were impressive, but the 10-foot-tall 300-foot-diameter raised mound and the 10-foot-tall stone walls with the woven walls and ceilings were amazing. It would be wise to remember how smart they were in the future, thought KO.

The celebration was fun. The Sasquatch danced, used hollow logs as drums, and sang songs that sounded like chanting and grunting at the same time. After hearing them sing, it became obvious they had a language, which was why Wally learned so quickly. The food was simple fruit, nuts, and various roots. It was apparent that the Sasquatch were mostly vegetarian, although they were known to eat fish and some birds. Wally loved smoked fish and would eat it until he passed out, so KO made a mental note to bring some up the next time he visited.

As dusk began to settle in, the Sasquatch came to say goodbye to KO and Wally. It was going to take a while for KO to get used to getting kissed on the top of the head by these giant beings. They are very gentle, and the kiss was a marvelous way to say goodbye, but their sheer size makes it uncomfortable. It finally dawned on KO that the adult Sasquatch only kissed his head and the heads of the Sasquatch children. Obviously, the adult Sasquatch looked upon him as someone small like their children. This might be one detail he leaves out when describing this encounter, thought KO.

KO slept on the mat with Wally and his family. To be honest, the Sasquatch were very clean and didn't smell, so sleeping with them wasn't unpleasant, except if one of the adults laid an arm or leg across KO. After days of travel and excitement, KO slept deeply and woke up snuggled with Wally and his little sister. After everyone woke up, they went outside to clean up in the pool set in the center of the clearing where they ate last night.

Everything was all smiles and happiness until KO brought out his mirror to shave. At first, no one noticed, but then the area erupted with chatter and excitement. The Sasquatch were all excited about the mirror. Immediately, a few of the Sasquatch went into their homes and returned, but each was carrying something. Once all the Sasquatch returned, they laid the things they brought back with them on a woven mat near KO's feet, then quietly pointed at their trades and KO's mirror.

It didn't take long for KO to understand. The Sasquatch wanted to trade his mirror for the things that they had brought. KO understood that trading was definitely a sign of intelligence and that these Sasquatch had a complex society. KO started looking at the trade items the Sasquatch brought and laid on the woven mat and was instantly awestruck. After seeing what the Sasquatch had laid down to trade, KO thought it was a good thing that he'd brought his backpack with him because he had plenty of things to trade for their trade items.

In front of him on the woven mats were an assortment of shells and wood pieces, but the coins, fancy jewelry, and what appeared to be gemstones interested KO the most. The Sasquatch obviously had no idea the human value of the things they laid down. For them, value was something shiny, pretty, or unusual. They had no use for money, but KO did, and these things would give him the needed cash to build his business, so KO started pulling things out of his backpack.

By the time KO was finished pulling things out, the Sasquatch were acting like they were having a party. They were dancing, chirping, and laughing because they knew KO realized what they wanted, but he surprised them with a windfall of wonderful things.

KO, put down two canteens, two each of spoons, forks, knives, three different sizes of metal pancake turners, a full metal cook set with two pans and three pots with lids. Then he added two metal cups, a metal coffee pot, and even a metal tripod for hanging pots for cooking over an open fire. Finally, KO laid down his metal boxes for holding spices, a medical kit, a small fishing lure box, and finally, two more mirrors.

The Sasquatch were beside themselves with all the metal, shiny silverware, and of course, the mirrors. KO lifted his hands over his head to quiet the Sasquatch down. When they were all paying attention to him, KO pointed at his things on the mat, then at their things, and shook his head, saying yes, then he backed up. He tried to let them know they could decide what to trade, and after a few of KO's tries, Wally stepped forward, spoke Sasquatch words, and made some hand signals. Then, the Sasquatch seemed to understand and began talking to one another.

Within a few minutes, each of the Sasquatch that had brought something to trade picked one of KO's things and stepped back. KO looked at the trade things he had gotten and was screaming inside, but knew the Sasquatch were just as happy. Not needing money would be a good thing, and the things he had just received in trade could make it so he never needed more money, KO thought, smiling.

KO reached into his backpack and pulled out his big old Bowie knife. His wife bought it for him, but the knife was too big to hold or carry. KO swears it must have been a display knife not meant to be used, and they sold it to her as a joke, thinking she would bring it back. KO decided to keep it because it cut wood pretty well when camping. It worked better as a sword in human hands. Anyway, he stepped up to Wally's dad, who he now knew was the troupe's leader, and held the knife out to him.

Wally's dad looked down at KO and gently took the knife in his hands. He slid the knife out of the sheath and held it up for all to see. The sword-size knife in KO's hand was a near perfect fit for an 8-foot-tall Sasquatch with oversized hands. It would be years later that KO and Wally could speak well enough together for KO to fully understand what an honor it was for Wally's dad to receive a knife that fit his hand. Sasquatch really don't need protection from predators, but like kids, especially boys, they like to cut and destroy things, so having a knife he could cut with was a great honor for him.

Wally's dad raised the knife above his head, spoke a few words, and walked to his home, only to return moments later. He walked up to KO, kissed the top of his head, and made a small laugh because he now knew that KO realized he only kissed the top of the head of the kids and KO. That was the first time KO realized how much the Sasquatch liked to play and tease. Then the huge hairy Sasquatch raised an arm above its head again, said a few words, and then offered the hand to KO.

KO looked into the Sasquatch's hand and literally gasped. The most stunning piece of jewelry he'd ever seen was in the huge hand. It was a necklace with so many diamonds and colored stones it was impossible to imagine. The chain was completely covered with gems and diamonds, and the craftmanship was beyond belief. KO was completely stunned and would have kept staring at its beauty for hours if Wally hadn't shaken his arm to make him accept the necklace. KO looked up at Wally's dad, bowed his head, and took the necklace out of his hand. Wally's dad bowed back and smiled. Then he kissed KO's head again and, this time, laughed out loud, and the rest of the troupe laughed as well, and so did KO.

KO put the rest of his trade booty into his backpack. The necklace was so fantastic it must be worth millions, thought KO, but the other trades were no less impressive. They traded gold coins and gemstones. KO was already planning the next trade trip as he packed his pack.

After trading, everyone gathered around and ate breakfast, or the Sasquatch equivalent, of fruit, nuts, and roots, like every meal they ate. KO decided he needed to introduce spices to the Sasquatch to improve their eating pleasure. Spices, silverware, napkins, or maybe let them enjoy their uncomplicated life. After eating, KO let Wally know that it was time for him to return to his home and family. Wally looked sad but knew that KO needed to go.

KO could ride the tide as he left, so he had an easy first leg, which gave him time to think. He wanted to trade with the Sasquatch so he could make money to build his business but he also needed to make sure he could protect the Sasquatch at the same time. Ormond Beach and the area around the Tomoka River were growing quickly, and it wouldn't be long before they wanted to build in Sasquatch land. KO needed to protect the Sasquatch, and the only way to do that was to buy all the property the Sasquatch needed and make it a protected preserve. Looks like he would be trading the Sasquatch for their own survival.

It took KO two full days to travel back home. A storm raised the water level and caused a bunch of wind, but the new boat performed flawlessly. He still wasn't sure how he was going to get his new Sasquatch treasure appraised without raising too many flags, but he needed to keep a low profile so the Sasquatch didn't get put in danger. These were his thoughts as he rounded the river bend to his cabin, when suddenly he saw his daughter, wife, Cooper, Wally, and over a dozen Sasquatch down by the dock having what looked like a party.

Everyone by the dock started yelling when they saw KO coming down the river. Two weeks ago, KO had never seen a Sasquatch, and now he had over a dozen by his dock, and his wife and daughter were playing with them like it was normal. It was a good thing KO didn't drink, or he might have thought he was seeing things and needed to stop. When KO reached the dock, Wally grabbed the boat lines and tied it up while KO went to see his wife, daughter, and over a dozen Sasquatch.

The first thing out of KO's mouth was, "Are you and Sandy ok"? Then he asked, "How and when did this happen"?

KO's wife and daughter and Wally hugged him, and the rest of the Sasquatch troupe came over to hug him. Sandy, Wally, and the other Sasquatch kids went off to play while the adults talked. His wife first told him she closed the gates to keep everyone out and hung a sign that said they were closed due to storm damage. Next, his wife told how she met Wally's mom and how she was the pregnant Sasquatch at the dock five years ago. She told how the troupe showed up yesterday, and Wally was able to explain they were waiting for your return for some reason.

Cooper was off to the side, sitting quietly with a very large Sasquatch. The two seemed to be quite content, sitting quietly side by side. Upon closer inspection, KO noticed the Sasquatch had as much gray hair as Cooper. KO's first thought was it was just two old timers sitting side by side watching the young uns play, and then his wife explained who the Sasquatch was. When KO heard who the Sasquatch was, he immediately went over to meet him. It took a few moments before Cooper and the Sasquatch realized he was standing there, and then Cooper immediately introduced KO to his friend.

Cooper told KO that this Sasquatch sitting here had walked up to him yesterday, pointed at where Cooper's missing foot should be, and shrugged. Cooper said he immediately knew that this was the Sasquatch that saved his life over 20 years ago when the giant alligator attacked and killed his fellow park rangers. With Wally's help, and the fact Cooper had been trying to learn Sasquatch from him while he was here, Cooper could thank his Sasquatch rescuer. For 24 hours, they were able to talk a bit, but mostly, they sat and watched the young ones play. KO knew meeting the Sasquatch that saved his life would help Cooper recover from the survivor's guilt he had always felt.

After saying goodbye to Cooper and his friend, KO walked back over to his wife, and she began telling him more of what happened when one of the Sasquatch brought out a wooden box that was 3-foot-long, 2-foot-wide, and 2-foot-tall. The box looked kind of like a pirate's treasure box, and the Sasquatch set it next to KO and opened it. KO's wife stopped talking mid-word when she saw what was in the box. It had been a pirate's treasure box at one time, but now it held the things Wally's troupe wanted to trade.

The box was holding pirate's treasure and some of the things the Sasquatch found that humans lost. There were some gold coins, but mostly the chest held jewelry and cut and uncut gems. Wally's father must have noticed how KO reacted seeing the jewelry versus the coins and loaded the chest with mostly those things. KO's wife was still staring open-mouthed while her daughter Sandy and a couple of Sasquatch kids came over to the chest and began playing with the jewelry and gems. KO looked at the chest, looked at his wife, looked at Wally, and signaled for him to follow.

KO grabbed a tool wagon and took Wally into the tool storage shed, where he kept the tools he had sold to the river people. KO loaded shovels, rakes, pickaxes, saws, hoes, buckets, pans, then brought Wally over to the main storeroom and loaded a box of metal signal mirrors, and a box of mess kits, and, best of all, a big box of canned smoked fish for Wally, all which was brought by the Boy scouts for a get together they had a few years ago, and these supplies were never used. KO and Wally pulled the fully loaded cart outside and dumped it next to the treasure chest the Sasquatch brought. The Sasquatch went as crazy for what they got out of the trade as KO's wife for the pirate treasure box.

KO knew the Sasquatch needed metal tools for keeping their village clean and plant-free. He also wanted to teach them how to do a bit of basic farming. They loved apples and nuts, so he was going to help them grow and cultivate them. While the Sasquatch examined the tools and treasures KO had laid out for them, KO pulled something out of his pocket and walked over to his wife.

As KO unwrapped the item he had pulled out of his pocket, he asked his wife to close her eyes and hold her hand out. KO unwrapped the beautiful jewelry Wally's father had given him two days earlier, placed it in his wife's hand, and then asked her to open her eyes. When his wife opened her eyes, they seemed to keep opening wider until KO thought they were the size of dinner plates. While she was still staring at the necklace, KO picked it up, put it around her neck, and said, "This is for you, and there's much more like it, so you better get used to it." Then KO kissed his wife on top of the head, looked at Walley's dad, and they both started laughing out loud.

## 8

---

# HUMANS AND SASQUATCH FOREVER

K O had a great plan to save these gentle beings. The treasure they brought would be more than enough to purchase the swamp the Sasquatch call home. There would also be enough to help the river people and, over time, introduce the Sasquatch to them. KO's plan was to buy up as much of the swamp the Sasquatch lived in as possible and make it a protected sanctuary so the Sasquatch never needed to worry about losing their home to progressing humans. The river people there would be able to stay and share with the Sasquatch.

Over the years, Sandy and Wally became great friends. In the early years, Wally came to play and learn English, and learn all there was to know about humans. Wally spent time with Sandy and KO as he got older, relaxing by the dock when he visited. When Wally's vocabulary got good enough, he eventually told KO and Sandy that his given family name was Gu, but he would always be their Wally.

Wally would eventually become the leader of his troupe, and

as their leader, he made sure humans and Sasquatch always played and worked well together. Over the decades, Wally, KO, and Sandy worked together to ensure the Sasquatch were protected, and they always remained friends.

# ABOUT THE AUTHOR

Patrick Talmadge Sr. has always been a late bloomer. His growth didn't cease until he was over 21 years old. He reached his pinnacle as a national and world-class masters middle-distance runner at the age of 37, when he won his first master's national track and field championship in the 800-meter run.

At 47, Patrick earned his Bachelor of Arts degree and made history as the oldest NCAA cross-country runner. Seven years later, at 54, he returned to college to pursue a Master's degree in Psychology. During this time, he ran the mile in track, once again setting a record as the oldest NCAA track and field runner. He received his Master's degree in Psychology at 57. At the age of 66, he embarked on his writing journey.

Patrick taught himself to read at the tender age of three and a half and has been an avid reader ever since. With a keen interest in all fields of science, science fiction, and fantasy, he amassed a wealth of knowledge that would later prove invaluable when he began writing. Throughout his 20s and 30s, Patrick devoured two to three books a day. Upon graduating from graduate school in 2011, he retired from competitive running and felt a growing desire to write the stories that had been simmering within him.

In November 2021, spurred on by the love of his life, Patrick began his writing career. By July 2023, he had completed an adult four-book science fiction series about Sasquatch, a four-book children's series on the same subject, and a standalone novel about a senior community that befriends a troupe of Sasquatch.

Patrick possesses a unique ability to write multiple stories simultaneously, allowing him to modify and adjust interconnected narratives for clarity when writing a series. With a bit of luck, Patrick will continue to pursue his passion for writing for the rest of his life, or at least until his computer gives out.

# ALSO BY PATRICK TALMADGE

# AFTERWORD

Go to hangarɪpublishing.com to learn more about the Authors and stay up to date with their newest releases.

www.ingramcontent.com/pod-product-compliance
Lightning Source LLC
Chambersburg PA
CBHW071546120626
46550CB00006B/2598